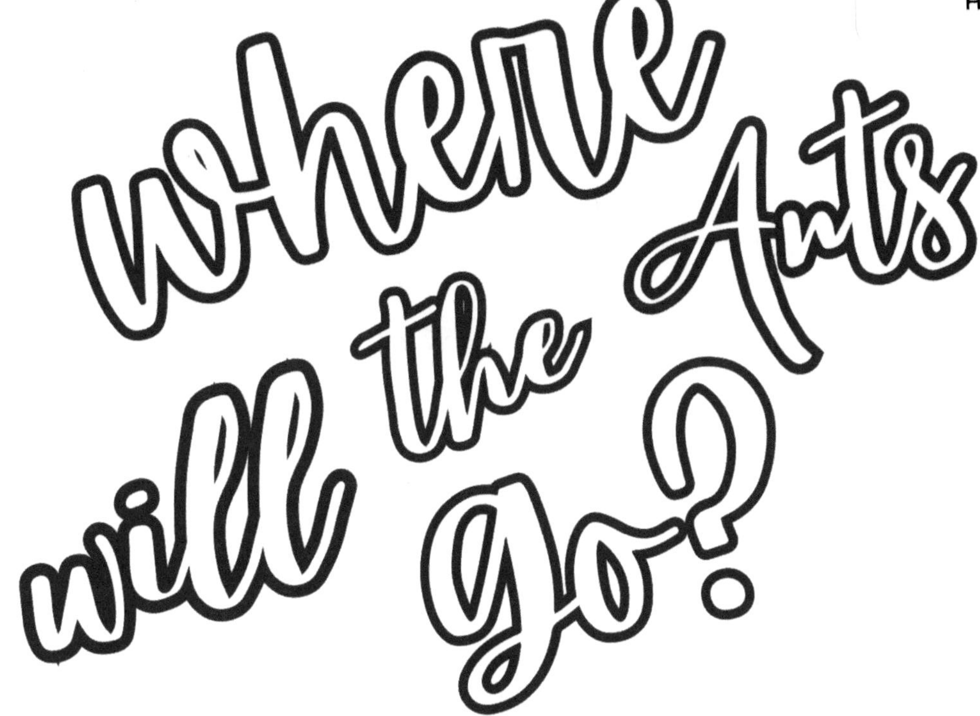

Where will the Ants Go?

Series- *Children's Nature Quest*

Author
M Borhan

From
Big 6 Publishing

Where Will the Ants Go?

"Where Will the Ants Go?" explores the consequences of deforestation and extreme land excavation on ant colonies. Deforestation disrupts ant habitats, leading to habitat loss, resource scarcity, and increased competition. Colonies face challenges such as altered microclimates, genetic bottlenecks, and disrupted mutualistic relationships with plants and other organisms. Extreme land excavation exacerbates these dangers, posing risks of collapse, displacement, and population declines. Ants must adapt to new environments, altering their nesting behavior and foraging patterns, while facing heightened vulnerability to predators and human-ant conflicts. These disturbances not only threaten the survival of individual colonies but also undermine the essential ecological roles ants play, such as soil health maintenance and seed dispersal.

Addressing these challenges requires holistic conservation efforts that prioritize habitat protection, restoration, and sustainable land management practices. By understanding and mitigating the impacts of deforestation and land excavation, we can safeguard ant populations and preserve the integrity of ecosystems they inhabit, ensuring a harmonious coexistence between ants and humans.

Let's get to know Ants' Life cycle first-

Social Structure and Division of Labor

Ant colonies exhibit a highly organized social structure, typically comprising a queen, workers, soldiers, and sometimes reproductive individuals (drones and princesses). The queen is responsible for reproduction, while workers perform various tasks such as foraging, nest maintenance, and caring for the brood. This division of labor ensures the efficient functioning of the colony.

Communication and Coordination

Ants communicate primarily through pheromones, chemical signals that convey information about food sources, nest locations, and potential threats. Through the release and detection of pheromones, ants can coordinate collective activities such as foraging expeditions and defense against intruders. Additionally, tactile and auditory signals may also play a role in communication within the colony.

Nest Construction and Maintenance

Ant colonies build elaborate nests that vary in structure depending on species and environmental conditions. Some ants construct underground tunnels and chambers, while others build nests in trees or use natural cavities. Workers continually maintain and expand the nest, removing debris, repairing damage, and regulating temperature and humidity levels to create a suitable environment for the colony's survival.

Adaptation and Evolution

Ant colonies exhibit remarkable adaptability to changing environmental conditions through a combination of genetic changes and behavioral flexibility. Over time, colonies may evolve traits that enhance their survival and reproductive success in response to selective pressures such as predation, competition, and habitat alteration.

what is happening to the Ants now?
Consequences on Ant Colony Habitats

Habitat Loss
Deforestation directly results in the destruction of ant habitats, including the intricate network of nests and foraging trails they establish in the forest. This loss of shelter and foraging grounds forces ants to relocate in search of suitable environments.

Disruption of Symbiotic Relationships

Many ant species form symbiotic relationships with Big Trees and other organisms. Deforestation disrupts these delicate partnerships, leading to a decline in the availability of resources for ants. For instance, ants may lose the Trees they depend on for food and shelter.

Increased Competition

As ant colonies move towards more urbanized or altered landscapes, they often encounter increased competition with other ant species or even invasive species. This heightened competition for limited resources can lead to population declines and changes in the structure of ant communities.

Displacement and Fragmentation

Deforestation fragments ant populations, isolating colonies and hindering the movement of individuals between patches of remaining habitat. This fragmentation can lead to genetic isolation and reduced genetic diversity, making ant populations more vulnerable to diseases and environmental changes.

Altered Microclimates

Forests play a crucial role in regulating microclimates. Deforestation disrupts these natural processes, exposing ants to harsher environmental conditions, such as extreme temperatures and humidity fluctuations. This can affect ant physiology and reduce their overall resilience.

Pesticide Exposure

In areas where deforestation is accompanied by increased agriculture, ants may face heightened exposure to pesticides. The use of agricultural chemicals can directly harm ant colonies, impacting their reproductive success and overall health.

Extreme Land Excavation

Extreme land excavation poses grave dangers to ant colonies. The disruption of intricate tunnels and chambers can collapse colonies, jeopardizing their structural integrity and survival. Additionally, excavation activities may crush or displace ants, disrupting their social organization and vital ecosystem functions, leading to population declines and habitat degradation.

Resource Scarcity

Deforestation often results in a scarcity of crucial resources like food and nesting materials for ants. The altered landscape may not provide the diverse array of plants and prey items that ants rely on, leading to nutritional deficiencies and population decline.

Increased Vulnerability to Predators
As ants move into new environments due to deforestation, they may encounter novel predators or face higher predation risks. Without the familiar cover of the forest, ants become more exposed and susceptible to predation, further reducing their populations.

Changes in Nesting Behavior
The loss of natural nesting sites in tree trunks or soil due to deforestation prompts ants to adapt their nesting behavior. Some species may resort to nesting in human structures, increasing the likelihood of human-ant conflicts and potential pest control measures

Shifts in Ant Community Structure

The alteration of landscapes due to deforestation can lead to shifts in ant community structure. Certain species may become more dominant, while others decline or disappear. These changes can have implications for ecosystem dynamics and functioning.

Stress and Colony Collapse
The stress induced by habitat loss and environmental changes can compromise the health of ant colonies. Prolonged stress may result in weakened immune systems, reduced reproductive success, and, ultimately, colony collapse, contributing to the decline of ant populations in deforested areas.

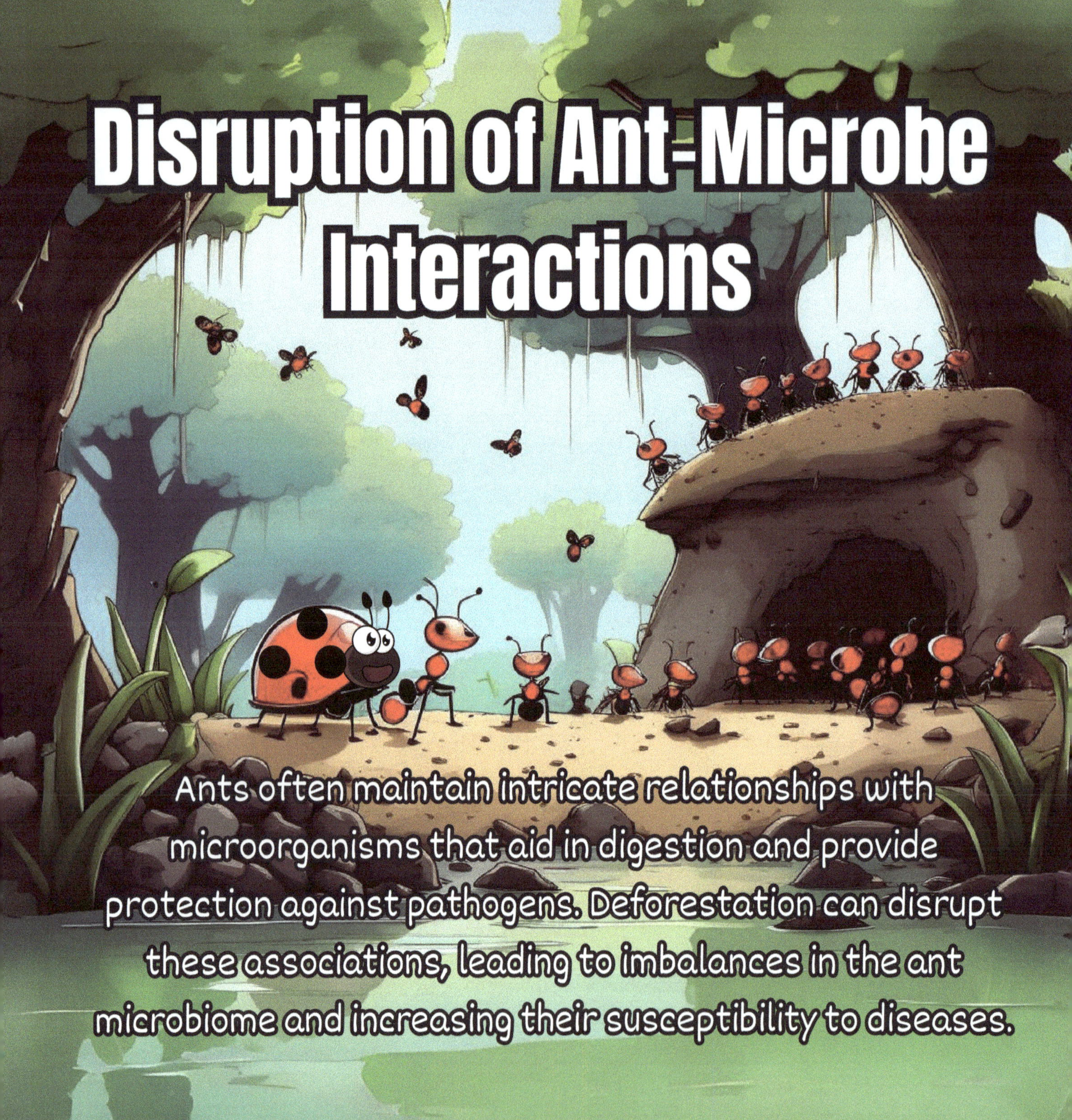

Disruption of Ant-Microbe Interactions

Ants often maintain intricate relationships with microorganisms that aid in digestion and provide protection against pathogens. Deforestation can disrupt these associations, leading to imbalances in the ant microbiome and increasing their susceptibility to diseases.

Genetic Bottlenecks

The fragmentation caused by deforestation can lead to genetic bottlenecks within ant populations. Reduced gene flow and limited genetic diversity make ants more vulnerable to diseases and environmental changes, potentially hindering their ability to adapt and survive.

Interrupted Ant-Plant Mutualisms

Many ant species engage in mutualistic relationships with plants, providing protection in exchange for food or shelter. Deforestation disrupts these symbiotic interactions, affecting the health and reproduction of both ants and the plants they collaborate with.

Disruption of Ant-Seed Dispersal

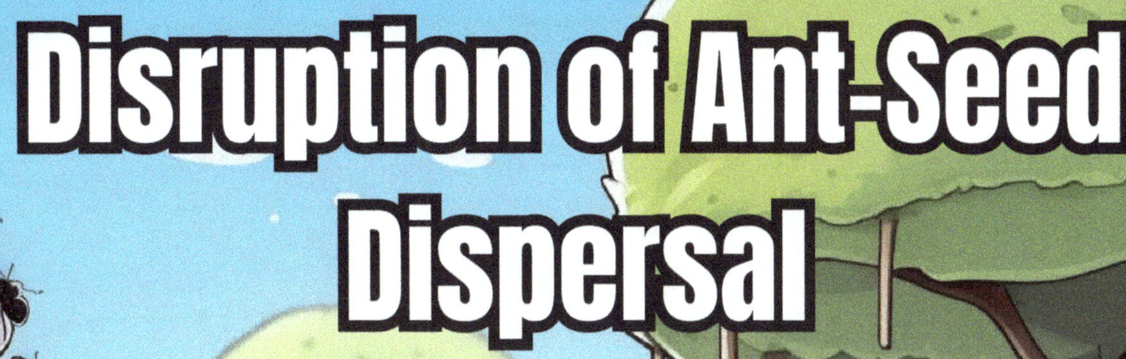

Ants are key players in seed dispersal, aiding in plant regeneration. Deforestation can disrupt this process, affecting the distribution and germination of plant seeds. This, in turn, can influence the composition of plant communities in deforested areas.

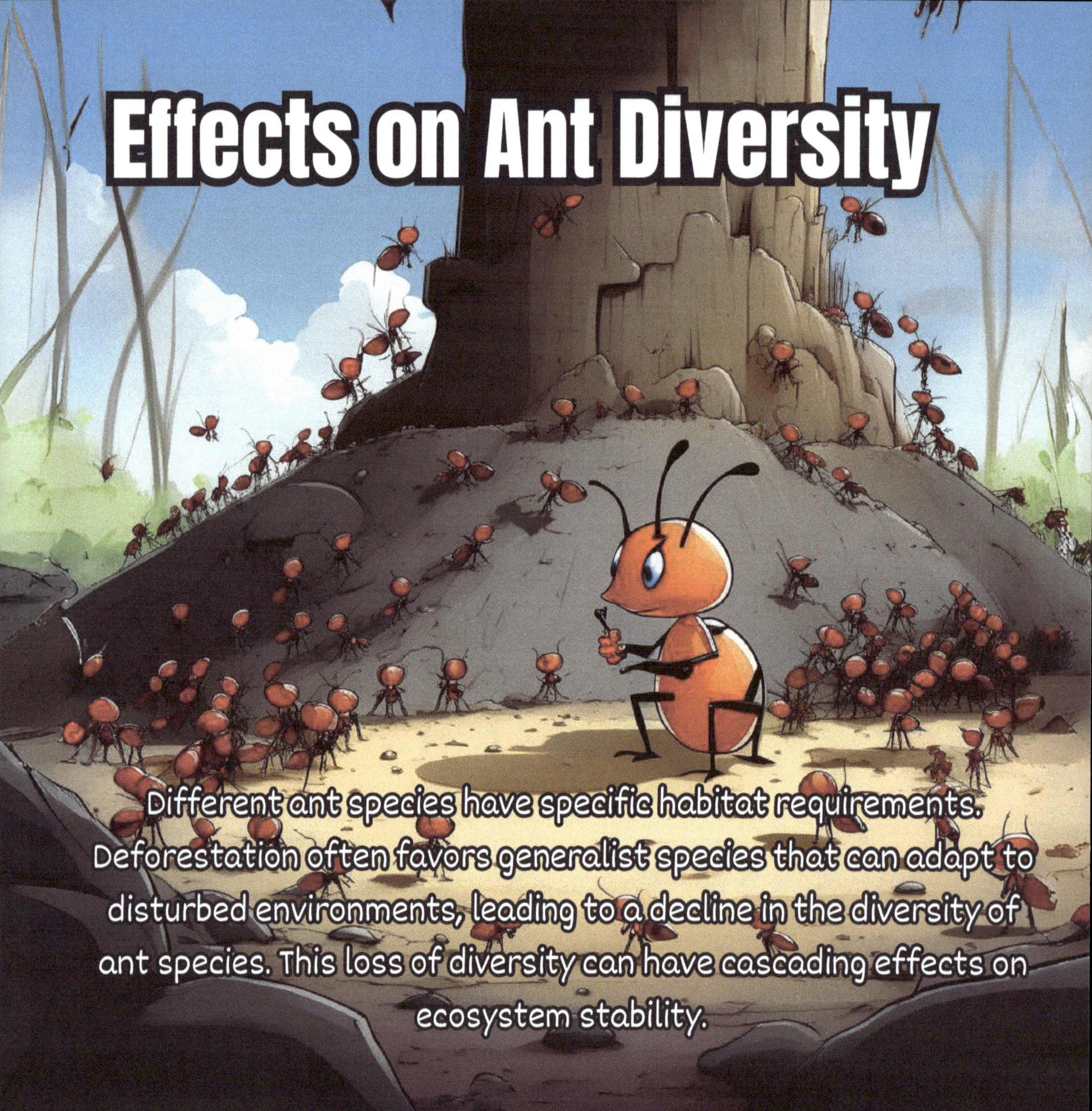

Effects on Ant Diversity
Different ant species have specific habitat requirements. Deforestation often favors generalist species that can adapt to disturbed environments, leading to a decline in the diversity of ant species. This loss of diversity can have cascading effects on ecosystem stability.

Role in Soil Health

Ants play a crucial role in soil health through activities like tunneling and soil turnover. Deforestation disrupts these processes, potentially impacting soil structure, nutrient cycling, and water retention, which can have broader consequences for the entire ecosystem.

So, What's the outcome finally?
Human-Ant Conflicts
As ants seek new habitats near human settlements following deforestation, conflicts may arise. Some ant species may become pests, invading homes and agricultural areas, leading to negative interactions with humans and potential pest control measures.